In the Space Between Songs

In the Space Between Songs

Poems by Carolyn Kesterman

Withopike Press

Cincinnati

The events in this book have been set down to the best of the author's ability, although some details have been changed to protect the privacy of individuals.

Copyright © 2025 by Carolyn Kesterman

All rights reserved. No part of this publication may be reproduced, distributed, or transmitted in any form or by any means, including photocopying, recording, or other electronic or mechanical methods, without the prior written permission of the publisher, except as permitted by U.S. copyright law. For permission requests, please contact the author: carolynkesterman.com/contact.

Cover Photo by Cat Rider

ISBN 979-8-218-65980-6 (paperback)

First Edition

Published in the United States by Withopike Press
carolynkesterman.com

*To Mrs. Wells, who told a
fourth grader that she should write a second story,
And to my parents, who agreed.*

Table of Contents

Part I: Winter

The In-Between 3

You Might Recognize Your Shadow in the Commas of My
Shredded Drafts 5

Prairie Fire 7

Still There 10

Downy 13

I Wish I Could Tell You I'm Sorry 15

Sometimes 16

What If 17

Bittersweet 19

In the Ink of Redrawn Maps 22

Respite 23

Each Time a Note is Added to the Score 24

Part II: Spring

Overgrown 27

The Trees Were Stained Glass Seas 28

Two-Hundred Ninety-Two Miles Upriver 30

Candid 34

Five Faded Syllables 36

Sage Green 38

Robin in the Arbor 40

Baby Face 41

Origins 43

Four More Circles 45

Echoes in Mine 47

Lookout Mountain 51

Wake 52

Part III: Summer

Electric Ghosts 55

Reckless Hymn 56

Freeway 57

Luster 58

Vanilla in My Coffee 59

Glitter 61

Someday, When It's Right 62

Choir of Bones 63

Entwined 65

The Ravine 66

Off the Edge of Yesterday's Map 70

Nowhere to Go 72

Detours 75

Drowned in Violet Embers 77

Unpacking 79

Part IV: Autumn

Caught Between the Silver and the Glass 83

The Hope 86

The Way It Was Supposed to Be 88

Margins 89

Spanish Moss and Longleaf Pine 91

Westwood 93

Cinnamon 96

Sonder 98

Without Saying It 100

Time to Turn the Page 102

Deer in the Snow 104

These Nights 108

Surrender 110

From the Space Between Songs 113

Part I: Winter

The In-Between

A cautious overcast sunrise reflected
Hot pink stars on the ceiling as it
Bounced off my college graduation balloon.
I tugged the string to make the patterns dance
Just to shift the sudden stillness in the room,
The silent beginning of a new semester whose
Syllabus was mine alone to write.

Three hours slipped by scanning listings for the
Perfect job and doubting every option.
Outside, the neighbor children shrieked on their bikes;
They knew which room they'd enter in the fall.
They'd have picture day and honor roll,
Predictable proofs of progress.
Their doorframes would be marked with the inches they'd grown.

As I closed the laptop to walk around the block,
Each milestone imagined seemed at least a decade away.
A house, a dog, a kid, a book –
Dreams too distant yet dependent on the present,
One unknown office building chosen out of thousands.

I relished the freedom, but cursed it, too.
I didn't trust my own hands on the wheel.

The horizon had never extended as far as it
Did those next two dozen seasons when I
Stopped defining stages as *first grade* or *senior year*
And started measuring time in flavors of coffee,
By emblems on the dash and marigold hues,
In albums on my shelf, the length of my hair,
The contacts in my phone and pens by the bed.

With thirty in my sights, you're holding the
First aforementioned milestone achieved,
Driven by the slow but steady progress in the dreaded In-Between,
Where the cadence of my heels on the marble of the skywalk is as
Restless as my sneakers were on asphalt –
Twenty-two, unemployed, with headphones in my ears,
Waiting for the next song to start.

You Might Recognize Your Shadow in the Commas of My Shredded Drafts

I wish I knew how to write music so I could
Fill the page with clefs and staffs instead of
Places all my friends would recognize.
I could strum the shapes of clueless eyes and
Hum the hues of paint peeling in plain sight,
Tuck regrets into eighth notes and
Forgive them with bridges too
Delicate to burn.

I wouldn't weigh the cost of pen names or
Find relief in rejected submissions,
Spared the sting of having to keep my
Best work hidden from everyone I know.
I'd let my aunts press play out by the pool
And swallow down the scalding inner critic
To watch my cousins' children dance to rhythms
Born from unsaid doubts I pray they'll never have.

These hands would never rest if they knew how to
Recycle empty worries into twenty silver frets.
My imagination would erupt at microphones where I

Wouldn't have to muzzle each creative impulse into
Vague and blurry metaphors
Or rewrite my life into softer, tamer chords.
There'd be less guilted deprecation,
Less humor forced into the cracks to
Dress up fragile dreams and foolish loves.

I'd make the strings confessors,
The drums, my stubborn pulse.
You could hear my pain without holding it.
I could give you hope without risking mine.

Prairie Fire

It's a Wednesday night and the week is
Stretched out on all sides like an endless field.
I walk to my room and close the door,
Draw the drapes on the dusk and
Twist the dials of my salt lamps.
My face is probably striking cast in pink, but
No one's here to see.
Lying across my bed, I turn on ambient flutes and
Flex my arms to force the tension out.
It's hard to convince my body that there's
No work left to do,
No reason not to trade the
Charcoal slacks and turtleneck for pajamas.

My hand hovers by my phone, but I let it fall and
Turn to the National Park posters that are
Framed beside my shelves.
The flute settles into a familiar place,
One I've known since ten when I
Wrote out a list of distant ambitions and concluded that

Galloping through hazy canyon sunsets and
Hills of crimson paintbrush
Should come second to nothing but the
New pursuit of story-writing.
Watching from my wall, these
Sandstone tapestries are as patient as they were when I
Sketched them there with my mind above
Sprawling adventures joined by stuffed bears,
Scenes punctuated with loose-leaf fantasies that
Turned into fervid oaths and incandescent chapters
Begging to be set loose on a
Wide and wondrous world.

But then, I was small and trusted a
Mythical, faraway grown-up would take me there.
Now, I am that woman and
Fear she is not enough.
There are too many responsibilities ahead of the
Bucket list in a hot pink binder.
It's beneath my bed and
No one's here to see it,
To promise what it's worth,

To run a hand over the page and whisper,

This summer – let's go!

There is only mascara being wasted on the sheets.

I replay the track.

It's a Wednesday night and my life is

Stretched out on all sides like an endless dream.

Still There

Is anyone out there?
I hear this question sometimes at night
In the space between my family's sleeping breaths and the
Ticking of my own pulse,
Alone with my face pressed against the
Cold pane of the side door
Where the shadows' sole response comes from the
Plastic candle that sits in the front sill of the
House at the top of the street.
I like to pretend it's real,
As if a true flame could keep
Warmer company than this dollar store bulb.
As if midnight didn't grip a fraction tighter
The week it burnt out last May.

My notebooks overflow with nights I forget to look.
Nights when my bedposts are painted silvery white with
Dreams caught on the underside of lightning or
Foregone writing memories to the moon.
Soft, inspired nights when
Padding sightless down a quiet hall can
Make me feel alive in a way completely removed of

Sunlit thrills and midday serenity.
Fleeting moments when the faraway rev of a motor
Whispers directly to me in the
Hushed tones of young girls at a sleepover
Sharing their blank-slate confessions on the basement floor,
A hum of energy charging the air,
Not from words,
But from the simple wonder of being witnessed after-hours,
Like all we paint ourselves to be
Is reduced to canvas in the dark.

But etheric revelations grow sporadic with age,
And inky black dreamscapes are
Easy to mistake for abandonment
When the day's drifted off without me.
Unobserved, I walk the halls and am
Deafened by the silence,
No comfort to be garnered from that
Sacred place of solitude,
Unable to romanticize the
Privilege of watching a world asleep.
I want to be seen.
I want to be heard.
I am alone and fear no one has known me.

So, lost, I wander to the side door to

Find the light at the top of the street.

And though my chest stays tight when I pull away,

It's enough to convince my body into bed.

Like that cheap but constant bulb is proof life goes on.

Proof someone will prepare a light for a

Place they won't see it.

Proof an unseen eye can be

Moored by our forgotten simplicities.

It won't inspire me in the morning like a

Two a.m. epiphany seized in starlight and snowfall,

But it will offer an answer to that prayer I risk for the sky:

Are you still there?

Downy

A sound I knew from playtime
Yet never before spied the source –
Quick, deep drumbeats
Traced across the frozen grass to a
Flurry of black and white feathers
Climbing, searching, digging
Into the bare, dead branches of the
Backyard maple tree where I
Used to build homes for my dolls.

Breathless, I steadied my elbows on the
Peeling side porch handrail and
Turned the camera dial to bring her
Bright spots and delicate barbs into view.
Higher, she journeyed,
Circling the hollowed bough in a
Graceful, weightless dance,
Sometimes hanging from her piercing talons,
Sometimes balanced on protruding twigs.

And when I'd taken a half dozen photos,
I kept the lens in place to simply watch.
Far enough away to give her freedom,
Close enough to sense the shift inside.

I Wish I Could Tell You I'm Sorry

I wish that lessons only stung the ones that learned them.
That it didn't take saying the wrong words to
Recognize their flaws.

I wish my careful sympathy cards weren't
Improvements on clumsier attempts,
That my allyship didn't bear the guilt of
Jokes I laughed at in middle school,
That my validations to a girl who'd been assaulted weren't
Haunted by the night I could barely speak.

I wish ignorance resolved itself with
Hypotheticals in classrooms,
That I'd never embarrassed frightened friends who
Deserved more experienced love.

I can't wish away the times I reached out to help and
Made things worse.
But I've learned that it's better to try than regret that I didn't.

Sometimes

Picture-perfect, you gave me your arm as the
Restaurant door closed behind us, and I very
Nearly laughed as I linked mine through and
Grasped your coat.
The downtown streets were uncharacteristically
Quiet as the snow collected on the pavement.
I blinked through the thick clusters of flakes to
Smile up at steeples and street lamp haloes, the
Bright white beams against a mauve night sky.
It doesn't dull the scene to say I called it off that weekend.
Sometimes a poem's just a verse.
The wind picked up as we turned the next corner,
And you tried to shield me from the cold.

What If

You keep saying I have a gift,
But what if I was just an average imaginative kid?

What if I had shelved the notebooks full of
Optimistic penciled escapes when I
Packed away the Barbie dolls and blocks?
Would I have entered the counselor's office without a plan,
Let her guide me someplace where
Years of hard work aren't boiled down to a
Desperate cover letter and five to ten sample pages?
Where the leap from pastime to profession
Isn't in the hands of an overworked scholar
Scanning a few thousand submissions for
Genius dressed in trusted tropes and themes?

I want to take a test drive in a life where
Adequacy doesn't have to feel like failure.
I want to know who I'd be if I weren't waiting for a
Dust jacket to validate the efforts,
The student debt,
The people who told me I could make it.

I want to know where my energy would settle
If I cut my future free.

You tell me the next agent might say yes,
But what if I just don't have what it takes?
What if I dialed this back to a hobby,
Let the drafts collect without sharing?
Could I justify the hours of enjoyment if I
Admitted that was all they'd ever be?
Would I keep penning daydreams with the
Destination off my back,
Or would the ink dry up as my time filled with
Things of better use and substance?
Would it be more mature to move on?

It's hard to walk away from the road I built my life on,
But it's harder to convince myself not to.
I'm tired of reading rejections.
I'm tired of dreaming alone.
I know I'll never see my name along a paperback spine.

But then again, what if I do?

Bittersweet

I push the broom past the cocoa and licorice,
Watching snow illumined by the parking lot lamps.
There aren't many of these nights left.
I can hear Pam and Doris make jokes as
They wipe down the counters.
Terri's singing along to the Beatles CD I brought in;
She laughs when Pam does the jerk.

I take a deep breath,
Trying to memorize the particular notes of
Chocolate I hardly notice anymore,
Though my family says they enter the house with me,
Embedded in my hair.
I know there will be a day when that scent will
Take me back to a time I'll call better,
Even if it's a time I have to outgrow.

I spent half an hour last Saturday
Perched on the high chair at the wrapping station,
Just studying the room –
The plastic snowflakes I hung from the
Ceiling tiles my second week here,

The counter's gold boxes tied in red ribbons I measure
Hand to elbow crook to hand.
I've seen so many people cross these floors.
Their faces blur into a singular tear.

None of this was expected.
Especially not how hard it is to leave.
I was supposed to graduate college and
Get a job in communications somewhere with a
Shareable title and byline.
I never would have written the endless summer,
The autumn that unraveled my hopes and
Led me to a candy store on Sweetest Day
Where small talk would open a door I'd
Never thought to knock on.

Has it really only been four months?
I've grown up so much with these women.
I have a feeling I don't even know how much yet.
Pam's given me a pair of dresses for work and
Terri's told me her favorite restaurant downtown.
They tell me I'm going to make them proud.
They tell me I already have.

I twist the broom handle to round the corner by the figurines.

Chris is closing out a register while the

Last customer picks up a box of the

Caramels Debbie loved.

The speaker says the road is long and winding.

I turn off the sign by the door.

In the Ink of Redrawn Maps

This time, I won't deny my youth.
There's a lot I admit I don't know,
A lot I learned too late.
If I could, I'd do it over,
Burn the midnight oil for another credit or dime
To stumble across that threshold
With more than this working draft.
But what's passed can't be retread,
So the only options left
Are to settle into lower standards
Or start filling in the gaps.
Maybe peace lies at the ends of shears and shredders
And in the ink of redrawn maps.
Whatever I've feared is missing,
I'll patch up for myself –
Practice the highways and read a little more
To close the distance to the next hope's league,
And possibly grow enough
To finally believe I have.

Respite

The gentle chimes of the creek bed's falls and ripples
Reached my ears in clear, distinct layers,
Uninterrupted by the dirt bikes and cicadas that usually
Pushed them to the background.
I stood beside the water for what felt like hours,
Studying the scene with my hands frozen in my
Coat pockets while my face absorbed the
Sun's first unfiltered appearance in twelve days.

I hadn't realized what was missing until I
Saw the morning's crisp expanse of blue.
Everywhere, the pale winter palette burned more
Vibrantly than summer's green,
Each simple stone and pine limb rendered bold by
Inspiration's absence.
I inhaled deep and didn't flinch at the cold.
The dark weeks were worth that single breath.

Each Time a Note is Added to the Score

Thursday night, waiting for the latest genius to
Drop new pearls of wisdom from his frozen shore.
Braced with anticipation like my life's about to change,
As it always does, in some small way,
Each time a note is added to the score.

The candle's lit, amber evergreen,
Reflecting in a half dozen crystals' druzy points.
I watch their fires flicker while the shadows goad my eyes.
If I make it to midnight, I might last through one song,
A taste of the keys next season could be tuned to.

In the fading hour, I recall the prior chord.
There's a final stroke of meaning in the smoke.

Part II: Spring

Overgrown

Would you take the untraced
Bounds of my spirit if I knew how to
Shed this misplaced shame?
My heart is wild and overgrown,
But I promise it shelters more than secrets and
Fosters more than words.
Dig past the tangle of
Far-flung hopes and visions left to roam –
Their boughs have wandered from
Deeper roots you may recognize;
They're the same I've seen in you.

The Trees Were Stained Glass Seas

Can children's eyes see extra colors in the sun?
There are memories I swear vibrate with
Hues I still feel but can't quite see:
Oak leaf confetti glittering down to
Trim embroidered cherries on half-buried lapels;
The backlit velvet of a buck's antlers,
Face-to-face on a ridge through Hopewell earthworks.

Sometimes I think I've found the
Imperceptible edges of the spectrum within the
Floating mirages of a summer morning,
Those drifting humid paths a child might
Mistake for evidence of spirits and angels.
Or perched atop the crests of crystal waves
Dancing over a cool Floridian lake,
Imaginary nymphs welcoming home a woman
As earnestly as they did to a girl.

I search the grounds of
Holy dawns and chromatic revelations,
But before nostalgia warms the scene,
There's often a split second of disappointment at the

Bleached-out, ordinary roads my past
Memorialized in sweeping, pulsing shades.

I've asked my friends, and they remember, too.
The skies used to stretch even higher.
The trees were stained glass seas.
We saw depths we only feel the ripples of, now.
We seek dimensions our memories suggest we can bridge.

Two-Hundred Ninety-Two Miles Upriver

Twenty stories high,
I steep my tea watching
Orange rays splayed across my river.
With 471 spilling towards the bridge and
Blue glass breaking up the levee,
It's hard to think of that steel-lined band
As the same rippling friend I
Learned to skip rocks in
Two-hundred ninety-two miles upstream.

My wanderlust may linger on photographs of
Multi-colored pebbles under
Wilder, clearer waters out west,
But no river could ever write itself into my soul
Deeper than my murky, overworked Ohio.
I was eight months old when my dad
Lifted me over his head to
Introduce me to a room full of
Historians, artists, and boat captains called the
Sons and Daughters of Pioneer Rivermen.
And from toddler to teen,
Septembers were a pilgrimage home.

Back over the bridge by the *Snyder*,
Through downtown Marietta
Straight off a Kincaid card.
We'd take our cases in the long way, past the
Sternwheeler Ballroom and Blennerhassett portrait,
To check in under the enormous wheel
Nailed to the ceiling of the Lafayette's lobby.
Then a minute after we'd seen our room,
My mom would rush to her board meeting
And my dad would take me outside.

I know there were rainy days,
But all my memories are of
Striking out for sparkling, glittering waves.
Before time lengthened my strides and
Skewed those hills smaller,
I'd have sworn that bend was heaven.
I used to fling pebbles with all my might,
Convinced they'd reach West Virginia when
My arms grew stronger.

What they never gained in distance, they
Earned through precision,
Copying my dad's low side-swing to

Taunt the laws of physics.

Seven, eight –

I don't know how many leaps they made.

We'd still be finding out if the

Banks never ran out of rocks,

Sending us back up the path to the

Ice cream stand and Riverview Antiques.

There was always a gray-haired man

Smoking in a chair beside the military buttons.

I couldn't tell if he worked there or not,

But the shop felt incomplete when

We returned my junior year of college

And the ash tray was gone.

Like the smell of Diane's perfume and the

Sound of Captain Stone's laugh.

The *Snyder*'s gleaming overhaul couldn't

Fill the empty chairs in the ballroom Saturday night,

And the calliope's echoes couldn't replace

Helen Prater at the keys of the lobby piano,

Inviting me to join her on the bench as she'd tell

Darlene and Bee and Gayle about the

Butterfly I drew for her ninetieth birthday.

The boats my parents fought for tickets on

Slowed their churning wheels into relics,
And the sons and daughters of those Sons and Daughters
Save their memories from land.

But out their windows,
The Ohio River still shines,
Rambling over the thousand rocks I
Slung from her shores and
Below the Lafayette doors I
Carried slide projectors from with
Floodwaters up to my third grade knees.
Under the flower baskets swinging from the
Creaking platform of the Harmar rail bridge and
Through the rusted frames of the
Glasses my three year old hand knocked from my
Dad's eyes into the Muskingum's mouth.
Two-hundred ninety-two miles past
Repaved landings and boats my mom could name,
To the feet of a concrete skyline and
Back into my heart.

Candid

There are drawers and boxes of photographs at home with
Yellow date stamps in the corner that
Claim they were taken a decade before I was born.
Every time Grandma tried to fix it,
Her camera reverted in a day.
So it became a signature, instead,
Evidence of who was behind the shutter
If you couldn't tell by the furniture in the background
Or the candor of the scenes.

Searching for a singular picture is never a quick task.
Shuffling through, my hands slow as I fall back in time,
The depth and color and texture of film a
Visual reminder of the divide between my
Digital present and those unhurried years.
I study lamps and frames on the wall behind the
Aunts and uncles she was focused on;
I can hear the birds around my cousin and me as we
Pedaled our training wheels down Gelhot Drive.
Further in, I disappear, and my parents' hair grows darker.
I watch my dad join my mom's brothers and nephews in

Bottle rocket fights, and I smile at images of my
Mom showing Grandma riverboats or playing her guitar.

There are a few years of our lives missing between the
Summer Grandma went to the nursing home
And the trip we finally bought a new camera for.
Memories of my preteens are confined to
Formal portraits for ballet and school –
I can't re-enter Papa's smaller house on Strawberry Lane or
Trace long-running jokes back to stills of my parents' laughter.
I'm not as certain how our faces looked from my middle grades to
High school when I took up where Grandma had left off,
Confusing then delighting friends as I
Captured our most ordinary moments,
The ones we miss the most.
The ones I write poems about.

Five Faded Syllables

I wear a pale yellow dress and
Swallow my anxieties for the sake of a scene,
One I'd have died to write in another life,
Back when the song I play across the bridge
Reminded me of you,
Though its warm, gentle chords were
Always more like me.

I find the table quickly; the years don't show on your face.
The first words out of your mouth after hello
Are to ask if I got taller –
You laugh that you remember me being a
Whole foot shorter.
Well, I wore heels back then, so I don't know.
You say a half hour later that I seem more confident.
I can tell it kills you not to know why.

Your brow furrows between animated updates, and you
Repeat with abrupt intensity that you
Really want to know what else I've been up to.
Everything I add confounds you more,
And I have to check my tone when I

Correct your assumption that I only have one friend.
I wasn't always so nervous and isolated –
You knew me in a global pandemic.

And maybe that's why your easy smile under the
Dim coffeehouse lights feels so disconnected from
The one I knew covered in masks or in pixels
When typed confessions felt like holding hands.
Maybe your name would never have
Ignited flares in my mind if I'd been
Hearing it out loud instead of reading it on a screen,
If we'd stood close enough to leave no room for my
Generous imagination.

Sage Green

The curtains in my room are sage green;
They match the woven blanket whose
Hue the shop called *fiesta* and the
Pothos leaves hanging off the
Carved antique table to
Brush the baseboard.

It's not the color I'd have chosen when I
Carried those vines home that March the office closed,
Five tiny clippings peeking out of the pot.
The world changed overnight, and I dressed in
Warm earth tones like a flower child,
Escaping from chaos in decades past as I
Edited spreadsheets on the porch.

A piece of me was still stuck in the sixties when I
Put my new bedframe together,
But when I went to choose the linens,
Old rock nostalgia felt too much like pretend.
A year and a half back downtown with
New friends and a busier schedule pushed the

Fantasies from my daydreams,
And let in a cooler, grounded hue –

Sage green, the color of the buds on
That mountainside trail when the
Rain had just ended.
I built a home around their potential and
Trimmed the walls with
Painted cliffs and streams.
Sage green, the shade of the
First breath of spring.
A whispered reminder to grow.

Robin in the Arbor

Robin in the arbor where April's soft purple
Tendrils of wisteria float over the
Bowed, weathered boards.
She grew up to the hum of cars on Sycamore.
Her sky has always been framed by glass and steel.
Small nest tucked into the branches,
Woven from the vines her grandmother rested on the
First day I came here on my break.
City unfamiliar, eyes ached for brown and green.
I heard the birds call the concrete *home*,
Same proud song as their cousins' in the woods.

Baby Face

I started pitching my voice lower last January
After I spent the day by myself and never once heard that
Tone they call a fawn response online.
It probably sounds a little sadder, now, but it gets
Less condescension from court clerks on the phone.

A coworker said today that I look older.
Most of it is makeup and a bit more confidence.
She gestured to my black sweater tucked into tweed slacks and
Said that I could pass as an attorney.
I'd just like to pass as twenty-eight.

Three years ago, a woman at the Plaza asked when my
Summer break was over, and she laughed when I told her my age.
The next day, I switched out the canvas backpack for my
Grandma's old black leather purse.
I wondered if it looked like I were playing dress-up.

It's funny – most of my friends get mistaken for being younger, too.
Everyone says we'll be grateful for that someday.
But lines are forming around our eyes whether or not they're

Still shaped like a child's.
I can hear my life's clock ticking at the same speed as yours.

There's a dress in my closet that I bought on sale last summer –
Black, narrow lines with twisted neck.
I'm waiting for the right event to wear it,
A day when I'm prepared to look my age.

Origins

Curiosity claims a lazy Thursday morning as I
Climb onto the half-wall bookcase to reach the
Walnut jewelry box atop its taller neighbor,
And I turn the bronze key to lift the lid.
It's been a decade since I thought to look inside it.
I pull out broaches and necklaces and try to piece together the
Lives I've learned from my dad's vivid stories –
The origin of our dark brown eyes in grainy memories
Gathered only from my birth to age three,
And the man I had to meet in photographs,
Their mutual passions for antiques and art scattered
Colorfully throughout the small chest.

Setting the top tray aside, I wander over cameos and a hatpin,
Her golden high school ring,
And I gasp as I lift out a yellowed cardboard box with my
Grandpa's elegant cursive scrawled in pen across the surface:
Garlan, jet adóre. Yours, D.
Inside rests a delicate bracelet inscribed with her full maiden name.
I wonder when and where he gave it to her,
What she said as he helped her with the clasp;

These details known only to them.

Though the ink offers answers to a different question –

Where the roots of these poems began.

Four More Circles

A car door is interrupted by a
Warm breeze thick with maple pollen,
And for a moment, the street skitters back into the
Minutely tilted scale of another spring when the
Morning joggers knew the color of my laptop and the
Robins hunted close.
I tense at my muscles' strain to
Coil back into shapes that fit the scene,
Like my body's a puzzle piece dropped in the wrong box.
Familiar chords and colors fill the gaps with
Unfamiliar distance –
How can four years change so much?

The wind shifts to pull the perfume from my neck and
Bind a woman to a girl,
Their differences stark but sewn deep.
I let the car door close behind me and type a
Message to myself in my phone:
If four years can change this much,
Then what's coming next?
Where will the birds become
Accustomed to my presence?

How many faces will I memorize whose
Eyes I've not yet seen?
Who's tasting the April air and
Looking through the hours
Back at me?

Echoes in Mine

I want to dedicate an entire book to you,
A whole shelf on the Somerville library wall.
There's so much poetry written in the
Ballad of your life,
Endless verses capping the
Coda that intertwined with my prelude.
Sometimes when the road forks ahead,
I can still hear the echoes of those notes
Ringing over mine.

Maybe someday, I'll fit the stations, ports, and bus stops
Into something broad enough to cover the miles
Yet concise enough to bind.
Like the two-page paper you shared with all your neighbors
When the other eighth-graders wrote
Essays on presidents and authors.
I wish I could have shown you the longer tribute that
Closed out my memoir course in college.
I think you would have liked the stories I chose.
Your laughter was so vivid when I
Recollected the day you accidentally drove onto the
Stripped blacktop of that construction site,

How the man in the bulldozer stared, slack-jawed
As you casually drove the length with a crooked grin,
A preteen girl cracking up in the passenger seat.

I've tried to write you something in the years since.
It's so much easier to capture the melodies
Buried in memories of your poolside chair or kitchen table.
Everything I start cuts short,
Drowned in reverent tears.
You stood too tall for that.
So I save your lessons for the private page and
Ration nostalgia to August tenth.

The best without you was five years ago.
You would have been one-hundred,
And I spent the rainy morning arranging photos
Into the shapes of the numbers.
There's a burn scar on my forearm from that evening
When I pulled your cinnamon cake out of the oven
With a little too much excitement.
I smile every time I notice it.
It's nice to be reminded of the summers at
Gelhot and Strawberry Lane,
Reminded to really look at the picture on my desk,

The one from your ninetieth birthday when
Everyone surprised you with cake and a
Ticket to visit home.
Someone in IT came to update my computer today and
Said you looked kind.
They recognized my face in yours,
And I didn't tell them you were my mom's stepdad.

It's an ordinary spring Tuesday, but the
Look in your eyes is speaking past the frame.
The cursor pushes further down the page as I
Imagine your answers to every question I type.
Whether you heard what I whispered in your ear that
Snowy afternoon while I chose pictures for your memorial video,
Or if you walked beside me into Pemaquid Harbor when
I cupped my hands to taste salt water for the very first time.
I wish I could ask the bigger things –
Names and dates and streets and songs.
Would you have boarded every ship if you had
Known where they would take you?
Were the destinations worth each labored mile?

That party hat grin says you'd do it all again.
It's a look I often find in the mirror.

I used to say, a long time ago,
That I wished I'd meet someone like you,
Until I realized I inherited what I sought:
Storyteller, helping hand, and jack of many trades,
Uncharted but never adrift.
Your ballad may be distant, but I
Still know every line,
And whether the words ever do make it onto the press,
I hope I always hear your voice echo in mine.

Lookout Mountain

You let me use your hairband so
Nothing breaks my view of the valley being
Painted orange and gold.
For forty minutes, we're sisters with a dozen strangers,
Wrapped up in fleece and wind-drawn tears.
My limbs should be heavy from these long days of hiking,
But they've never felt lighter.
Dried thistles break the air and cast their
Shapes on amber cliffsides.
Everything is still and all is sweet.

Our neighbors applaud as
Saturday slips behind the mountain;
Blankets are rolled up and cameras closed.
You laugh and drag me by the waist when I
Take my twentieth look back.
It's okay to go – I've left some of my roots in these rocks,
Down the cliffs, through the caverns,
And in the pools of each cascade.
We leave more along the mile walk back to the car,
Two tourists finding respite from our quarter life crises,
Disrupting the mountain's peace with our own.

Wake

Our axis slowly tips homeward,
The corners of my smile stretching with the days.
I greeted Spring, expecting her to
Whisper ballads in my sleep like before,
Wild visions that cleared another winter's fog and
Spurred me on.
But the date of the night that once
Clipped line breaks into my prose
Rolls past without strings or fire,
As if to remind me of what this year has already said:

The dream has played.
It's time to wake.

Part III: Summer

Electric Ghosts

It's two in the morning and this
Week's been so painful, I should
Kill the music and sleep.
But wandering in the dark to the kitchen,
Thunder rolls through my bones and
White flashes splash time across my skin,
So I pad to the side door to invite chaos
For the second time this week,
Fresh melodies fading into
Drumming sheets of wind and water
As a crack of life splits down the sky and
Shoots up my spine,
Electrifying ghosts I didn't know I'd forgiven,
Wading into that womb of light and shadow
Where fear has the courage to
Become something greater,
Where wrecks of our past misfortunes
Hold hands and promise their surrenders
For so long as our hearts can withstand
The potency of being free.

Reckless Hymn

Crack the code from root to marrow;
I want to feel the pulse of heaven beneath my feet.
Up these cliffs are hymns only the reckless know,
Sweeping, jagged notes that rise and spiral so easily
You'd swear they were played by hand.
Heartbeats stretch up here.
Hours roll into seconds,
Where you can reach into the ether
And riffle through the atoms of a breath,
Impressions pressed into possible lifetimes,
A dreamer's road beckoning
Between the haloes of golden hour pines.

Freeway

My first published prose was an attempt to
Capture the hoarse romance of
Gas pumps, pop bottles, and
Amber skies that stretched my
Restless soul out to its proper size on
Days when escape was my best hope and
Farthest dream.
I laughed to keep from crying the
Afternoon my dad played the Eagles at the
End of my first on-ramp –
Old teenage daydreams merging into the
Trembling but very real hands on the wheel.
I had feared the highway would
Dazzle me less once my pulse met its speed,
But if it lost any magic,
It was only in its transition from
Fantasy to truth,
The ache in my limbs as artfully raw as the
Steel canopy murals of rust and oil that
Promised freedom to a girl who
Should have known she held the keys herself.

Luster

A hundred miles melted at the familiar
Textures of your voice falling gentle and
Clear over the flushed crowd like the
Late autumn snow you took us to
In the middle of a green midwestern field.
The last few beams of twilight touched the
Backs of outstretched hands as you
Bowed your head to feel the second verse.

In a sentence, I forgot the road to get here;
One word dispelled the awkwardness of walking in alone.
Your face dissolved into luster as our
History filled my eyes,
Eleven months of repeating those lines like mantras –
Blue hour highway on a different summer night,
Holding hands through the speakers with a stranger.

And as my vision cleared to bring the final
Chord change into focus,
The floodlights caught a salt trail mirroring mine.

Vanilla in My Coffee

Those privileged white girls and their lattes, he ranted on a
Thursday morning in June, and I'm mad as hell to say I laughed.
Maybe it was simply out of kindness to a friend, or some
Need to show up smart and worthy to the
Self-diagnosed stoic stirring intellect into his
Chain-store cappuccino.
I grinned through the creeping apprehension as he
Continued, mocking the crystals he said girls bought to
Ignore the emptiness left from learning they
Weren't as special as their parents had claimed.
The heat rose to my ears when he explained how they
All lived in sugary, plastic delusion,
And though I found it hard to shake my head, it was
Just as impossible to nod.
My eyes may have been freed from shadow in that brief hippie phase,
But four years of girls' school were scored like
Pledges on my core – promises of
Sisterhood and permission to express humanity with
Pink and blue and basic black alike, or with the

Amethyst next to my salt lamp that I've since joined with others –
That day, a private, uncomfortable secret as I
Laughed again at his jokes,
Hoping he wouldn't smell the vanilla in my coffee.

Glitter

Smiling, I wash rose gold stars from my left arm
Where I held onto you all night as
Flashes of our shared adolescence
Soared and crashed over a flood of
Off-key soprano communion clad in
Sparkling reflections of each other's light.
Had that field ever witnessed such love?
No side pitted against another,
No roaring cries for anything other than the
Impossible thrill of hearing the
Private score of your youth sung out loud,
While seventy thousand screaming echoes
Prove, a decade late, that those girls were never alone.

Someday, When It's Right

It'll be like the first time I saw the ocean –
Really saw it, that is.
Not the glimpse in the distance at the end of the harbor,
But two white, rolling waves past the lighthouse lot
Where eight gasps drowned out the
Professor giving context to the site,
Seatbelts clicking free as we leaned across one another to
Crowd the starboard windows of the van.

Every sense overflowed as I descended the rocks,
The salt and sky and sea spray replacing the
Restless noise, the simple worries,
The unachievable quest to be enough.
I didn't touch my camera when a gull landed beside me,
Or when a swell crashed into a boulder,
Tossing Pemaquid high in the air.
I stared, I drank it in;
A weight I'd never noticed dissolved in the foam.

It wasn't like I'd imagined it would be.
I didn't cry or race toward it in excitement.
I walked slowly, deliberately, down to the shoreline.

Choir of Bones

Pull the languages of our ancestors from the
Marigolds bound across your wayward path.
She awaits you.
From the days you strung clover into crowns,
Her answers have been promised on the wind.
You've heard her when the moon is full.
You've joined her dance on the water.

Every time I abandon her mysteries for logic,
That song returns in the form of a dappled sky,
Pushing my pen with or without my aid.
She'll draw beauty from the deadest cells.
She knows where the wick stays green.

Under a kaleidoscope of stars,
She recounts the harmonies I'd forgotten,
Timbres bright in my blood.
This wandering choir of bones,
A transit for the history of the human race.
In our most magic moments,
We are the rhythm and the verse.
We are the breath between notes.

Close the miles and lend your tears to the descant.

Shed your fears and caution to show us the

Visions you slip into after work.

Ride the tremulous bonds bridging what was

And what fantasies you were born upon

To sculpt a midsummer dream you can sink your teeth into.

Graphite and tea.

Bare feet on the porch.

There's everywhere to go and endless roads.

Someday you'll take them all.

Somehow you already have.

Entwined

In a golden hour prophetically diffused by the
Passing smoke of a late July wildfire,
I bent beside the fading lavender bush for
One last inhalation of summer's potent glory
To discover a strand from my stubborn blonde streak
Woven into its remaining blossoms.
Apologetically, my hands reached to pluck it away
Like it were a choking weed or crumpled wrapper,
But with another breath, I watched it sway with the branches,
Saw the bees rest beside it without complaint,
So I leaned once more to sample the season's most fragrant gift
Before turning back to the porch with
Three years of sun-bleached growth left behind to
Join the gentle petals in the earth.

The Ravine

Two blocks from this window, my dad hooked the
Chain back onto his childhood swing
To keep me entertained while he pulled English ivy from the
Bricks soon to go up on the market.
In all the time I'd spent there,
Playing with blocks and helping him paint baseboards,
That metal seat had hung down in the grass,
Taunting me from the edge of the clearing I'd been warned to avoid
Since the day he'd driven the lawnmower over a
Particularly formidable ant hill.
They're gone now, he assured me, when he saw me eye the mound.
I nodded and sat gently on the seat like it were paper.
It's funny how the forbidden is rendered divine.

I leaned back to set the steel chains into motion, and their
Faintly eerie screeches turned the scene into a movie.
Forgotten keys in music boxes – I'm sure you know the sort.
I was fascinated by old things,
Specifically old things that were secret.
The higher I swung, the bolder the imaginary grew,
Until the miniscule flutter of gnats' wings turned to
Pixie dust in the rays,

And my eyes repeatedly tripped upon a gap in the tree line
Where my dad had once taken me, years before –
A narrow, hilly footpath to another family's backyard,
Perilously muddy and littered with abandoned carts.

When his shears finally paused, I hopped off the swing to
Ask if we could take the trail after lunch.
Yes, he started to say, then looked again at my expression,
And, with a knowing grin, he assessed the slope and
Told me to stay on our side.
It's difficult, twenty years later, to comprehend the
Largeness of emotion in that relatively simple taste of freedom,
But while many other memories from that year have faded,
I can still feel how my heart raced blazing that
Forgotten line through rag weed and honeysuckle.

The woods were much kinder than the junk heap I remembered.
If I could reenter the scene with today's perspective,
Perhaps I'd find that the shopping carts had merely been
Covered up by vines, and that my nine-year-old imagination had
Brightened all the colors of her storybook illustration.
I wouldn't go back there if I could.
I wouldn't want to find that I'd exaggerated a thing.
Not the height of the boughs nor the length of the ravine,

Where a bright yellow rope hung down
From a tree on the opposite ridge.

Recent shoeprints appeared on the path as I
Descended into the weed-covered gully and climbed the other side,
Yet awareness of the neighbors' proximity
Didn't squelch the sense of magic in the clearing.
I approached the rope like a timid deer and studied its source above,
Picturing the tall, intimidating boys who must have
Climbed such an impressive height on such a precarious ridge
To tie a rope so they could swing like pirates over a
Sea of ferns so dense it was impossible to perceive its depth.
The magic started to die as I envied their strength.
Maybe more than that, their nerve.

Continuing up the hill, I found the daredevils' house,
So I turned to make my way back.
But passing that tree and the yellow rope
Waiting patiently above the ravine,
A choice opened up to a place where my shy obedience
Rarely ventured.

There were countless flights that summer and the
Next spring when the realtors closed the deal,

But there's only one I really remember,
One that sometimes flashes back into focus at
Heart-pounding heights and spine-raking risks –
That first step off the ledge that sent me
Soaring, then gaping, wide-eyed and breathless when I
Felt both my feet stick the landing.
I'd honestly expected my dad to discover me
Unconscious in the deep abyss of leaves.
But I'd known as I carefully shuffled to the edge and
Wound my fingers through the split neon braids –
If I chose in that moment to walk safely away,
So would the woman that I'd someday grow to be.

Off the Edge of Yesterday's Map

August's mirage shines up ahead through the
Late hour gilding the pavement
As I push the edges of yesterday's map,
Fumbling over lyrics to
Refrains I laugh off-key.

It was supposed to be a short drive, but now I'm
Halfway through the album and I
Just passed the exit Papa took
That day he taught me how to find your
Peace of mind by getting lost.

It's a flashbulb in my memory –
The layers in his tone as he
Acknowledged the caretaker's toll,
The need for momentary respite from
Responsibilities I knew he'd

Choose again no matter the
Cost of golden years.
How the weights and walls dissolved when I said I

Understood and that I didn't mind
Staying out longer.

I can see his creased hands spinning the
Wheel somewhere aimless.
My own tap the signal for a road I've never taken.
The horizon's growing pinker in the rearview,
But I still have eight tracks to go.

Nowhere to Go

When idle hours became a prison and I'd
Walk just to move and see something other than
My potential passing by,
An August afternoon took me to Epworth and the
Brick and ivy houses that
Bordered my blue ribbon high school
Back when every step was directed for the next degree
Without a thought for the stagnant months after the
Last honor cords are packed away.
I pressed on past the edges of my memory's map
To side streets narrower, quieter, and denser with trees,
And in a rolling, piney side yard,
My eyes locked with those of a teenage deer.

Not a single other soul was in sight;
There was only the distant sound of
Tires on Harrison Avenue a couple blocks beyond.
I almost pulled the phone from my pocket to
Document the precious minute in a
Dull, monotonous summer,
But it would have broken the magic.
Quick double blink, flick of an ear;

We kept each other's company until her
Family stole her away,
And just when the clouds had cleared inside my head,
The ones above released.

I eyed the wide porches with envy as my
Shoes filled with rain and a stranger peered
From his living room drapes with
A bit more judgment than concern.
I wondered what I looked like,
What a smarter, smoother person would do in
This situation they'd likely never fall into,
But the wind drew waves and spirals
Across the puddles at my feet,
And somewhere in the mile,
Agitation drowned in inspiration.

I unlocked the door with a shiver at the indoor air and
Shuffled down the hall to hang my
Dripping clothes by the vents and
Wash the rain from my hair.
I remember I was singing as I unfolded the
New green sweatshirt I'd bought at the
Puffin's Nest in Damariscotta where I'd

Earned three history credits the summer before,
And while the chill of my misadventure settled into the
Soft, thick layers of a pine-hued daydream,
I rewound the hour to trace the lines of the
Tawny ears and jet black eyes,
Crisper in my vision than any camera could provide.

I searched for an angle to pull the image into fiction,
But there was nowhere to go with the protagonist,
Aimless and naïve any way I turned her.
There was no conclusion to her story,
Like the four pages I'd drafted earlier that week about an
Honor student who hooked an
Ounce of leftover achievement
By replacing the bulb over the kitchen sink.
So I shelved the afternoon carefully beside the
Sunburn I'd gotten on my way to the library and the
Cherry slushie I'd splurged on at the gas station,
Paused mid-scene until the morning I
Turned onto Lischer five years later to see a
Pair of does exiting the woods by that same rolling passage,
And understood why the meaning had to wait.

Detours

The Ryman thundered from balcony to floor as the
Audience smacked the backs of the pews in front of them,
Begging the band for the encore they all
Knew was coming, but pleaded for, regardless.
I memorized the sound as I struck the oak, and
Turned to look at both of you.

Tuesday had ended in tears.
I'd interviewed for a position I wasn't convinced I even wanted,
And as I squinted into the future to
Determine where my life had to go,
There was no clear path, not even a
Tidy, poetic fork in the road –
Everything was faded and blurred.
As I unzipped my suitcase and folded in my clothes,
I swallowed down the bitter regret that I'd
Ruined the trip I'd been looking forward to ever since I
Risked hitting send on the suggestion
Eight slow months ago.

Thursday afternoon in mid-July, we skirted
Construction in downtown Nashville, detouring

Two blocks over and one block back in the
Blazing summer sun;
Centennial Park had an awful lot to live up to.
But along the hours lost on side streets that will
Never make it onto a gift shop postcard,
I collected a hundred snapshots in my mind which would
Wander into my daydreams more often
Than the band's immaculate set –
The railroad tunnel your cinematic instincts gravitated toward,
The parking garage where we cooled down and bought some water,
The enormous tree we collapsed under
When we finally reached the park.

My hair was still damp from our curative hour in the
Hotel pool when we crossed the tracks once more.
A few silver clouds broke the rich, gold light into
Long, discernable facets on the sky.
We stopped to take a photo before descending into the Gulch.
And halfway down the stairs, I
Chanced another peek ahead and felt
At ease with the unmarked map.

Drowned in Violet Embers

Throw your torn-up sketches onto the
Pages I've ripped from this book.
We've carried their secrets long enough.
Let's strike a match tonight for every
Soul that pulled us up, and let the
Light guide us further from the rest.

Show me where their
Arms weren't there to catch you.
Lead me deeper through the
Ruins you've disguised.
I'm ready to share half of yesterday's weight
If it frees up your hands to touch tomorrow.

Dive in, ask me anything you
Need or want to know,
Just bear with me – the story may be
Stilted, but it's yours.
Read these scribbled truths and lend me
Ink to write another.
Convince me that my life is still on time.

And somewhere in the night, we might
Forget what we were burning.
The past might drift above the smoke and ash.
We'll strike another match for all the
Scraps we've spun to gold,
And watch the shadows drown in violet embers.

Unpacking

The road still rang in my ears that
Sunday afternoon I opened a chapter to proofread,
Keeping my midnight rooftop promise to a fearless pair
To nudge yesteryear's efforts to the shelf.
But I'd barely scanned a paragraph before
Tennessee's certainties and contradictions
Filled the room like the
Hundred bands of Broadway Street,
All belting out their myriad passions in
One ferocious disharmony.

So I opened a fresh page to
Peel back the months like they
Belonged to an old friend –
Holding hands with every indecision and
Clearing space for new ones ahead,
Slowly typing the kinds of questions and answers a
Midsummer's day has been known to elicit –
What it meant to be wild and whether
Maturity were synonymous with surrender,

Whether the stars should or could stay in the sky
Rather than gracing artists' eyes,
And whether the muse were
Never dead but merely dormant.

Part IV: Autumn

Caught Between the Silver and the Glass

There were prayers I pressed into the ground
Beside the pale pink dianthus,
Taking caution not to snag what
Time had buried in the fall.
Whether their ambitions took root with the rest or not,
That summer was destined for growth.
The returning daisies welcomed the bee balm as the
Garden borders tiptoed out beneath the trowel.
I gathered the weeds with patient hands and
Promised to tend the Susans
A louder, distracted August never
Granted a second bloom.

The soil underfoot was rich with plans –
Books to read and roads to learn.
I traced out the blueprint with my spade.
I'd clip lavender to hang in bundles
From the window latch above my bedframe,
Keep a notebook and a pen near the door.
I'd wring July of old storms and
Pour justice into June, where
Sage green folk songs would unweave the

Winter's restless dreams and
Rock the paper refugee in me to sleep.

Laughter with strangers,
Vanilla in my coffee,
Candlelit poems tucked beside pressed wisteria.
I cut my hair like it would matter;
I bought a yellow sundress when it did.

In another age, when all my steps were
Reserved for a softbound destination,
I'd sometimes look up from the oil-worn keys
To gape at the clock and word count –
My work was never better than when my
Heart leapt past the cursor instead of
Scanning its trail.

Amidst the falling leaves, I looked down to find
Exactly what the spring had planned,
Now far from that season's hopeful seeds.
The clumsy shoots I'd nurtured had
Climbed into steadier, confident boughs,
And the roots I'd once taken pride in

Were hidden deep beneath.
I wondered what I'd traded in to get there,
If I'd lost the original vision somewhere in the
Single-minded effort just to grow.

All passes; change is constant –
These thoughts aren't new, but they bleed.
So I dipped my pen in them and freed the verses
Caught between the silver and the glass,
Measuring the miles gleaned with
Lines cast from riverbanks where I learned to walk
To mountain cascades where I learned to stand.

And as I dug up the geraniums and
Cleared the dying weeds,
I pressed one last prayer into the cool, dormant ground:
That I might recognize which dreams were
Designed to return next spring,
And find the space somewhere to sow a thousand more.

The Hope

I debated walking down a stranger's driveway to
Avoid catching up to the car stopped at the light.
But I kept my head high and didn't slow my pace
While they provided Part II of a speech I won't repeat.
It's been happening more since last November.
Though I'm less afraid of those uttering threats
As I am of how they've changed me.

Somedays, I have to clench my jaw to
Keep from shouting back.
The fuse isn't new, but it's never been this loud.
My skin is crawling as I read the morning news;
I want to scream when I see the phrase *her place*.
I don't want to be like this.
I don't want to turn into something angry.

Liz said my trademark as a writer was the Hope.
I used to sneak the word *dream* into every story.
I used to believe in a future as diverse as the
Picture books I was raised on,
As innovative and green as the
Posters in my classrooms,

As welcoming, as respectful, as I was taught to be.
I used to believe in a future, but now...

Please don't take that away from me.
I never wanted to be naïve, but I
Desperately wanted to be kind.
I don't know how to write anymore if I
Can't end the page with a promise.
It's hard to pull my chin up long enough
To tell you that somehow, we'll make it.
It's harder yet to stay silent.

The Way It Was Supposed to Be

This isn't the way it was supposed to be,
I write, then tear the page from
The binding to crumple it deep into my
Purse to throw away inside.
Some moments don't need to be captured,
Even though the headlights whispered to the
Snowflakes and the sky sighed a
Heavenly gray I swore was touched by
Lavender, the same shade my
Sleeping ears processed from the call button tones
That morning I stirred and asked the nurse what that
Beautifully melancholy melody was – a child
Dreaming through the storm, but maybe
Just an artist, an artist doing anything to
Turn the pallor into palette where the
Days between tears and laughter could
Etch themselves into broader vistas, longer miles,
And the poems all circled back into what they were
Supposed to be.

Margins

I've spent eight years trying to
Summarize the sweet grief
Of dried pine needles stuck
To the bare heels of my feet,
But prose doesn't linger on
Thick swatches of forest green.
It can't begin to scratch the
Surface of time lost in
Diagonal rows of light
Dashed across the
Afternoon floor.

I can't capture this collection of
Moments inside a louder plot,
One that reduces the smell of
Cantaloupe and coffee to
Scene development of Chapter Three,
That chains symbolism to the
Nebulous ties between
Mallard wings and tortoiseshell glasses,
Or casts foreshadows

Over napkins tied into
Mice at the kitchen table.

I see verses waiting in the
Folds of lace curtains and
Wish I were apt enough to
Honor them.
The places where I used to
Step back to summer are
Fading away.
They're painting over shutters and
Tearing down the walls you
Used to watch me climb.
But I can close my eyes and

Picture you there.
I can cut loose the plot to
Find you in the poetry.

Spanish Moss and Longleaf Pine

Spanish moss and longleaf pine –
Her eyes reflect the full September moon.

"*Alive*," she whispers with her hands stretched flat over the
Cool, rough wood of the balcony rail,
Like she wants to know the curve of every grain.
A boat glides through the silver waves with a
Short, low call to the docks just out of sight;
The silent response is as soft and gentle as the
Lacy silhouettes of moss swaying in the breeze,
The fine wisps of her widow's peak straying from the
Heavy remnants of a late night swim
To dance in the moonlight and kiss her cheeks.

"*Alive*," she whispers, as she has since she
Rested against the rocks of the falls,
Heart wide and full in the
Deep amber lamplight of her childhood.
The same light she saw in the
Chords of sweetgrass love songs and the
Scent of burning wood.
It covered her limbs in the water,

Soaked through the years and all the summer's scars
To reach a place no storm could touch.

"*Alive*," says the lake as she pulls back the door.
The boat announces its arrival home.

Westwood

The boughs on Werk and Epworth plunge the berms in ruby flames,
And the rusted wrought iron fence is kissed with gold dust.
October's charms push me deeper into the maze of brick and stone
Whose weathered sills and green, globed lamp posts once coaxed
Secret Garden fantasies from my backseat view,
When diamond panes and ivy spoke of old, mysterious treasures,
Like the Victorian tower I watched chip away among her
Ancient, reaching trees and tawny grasses.

I've walked past this sprawling estate since the
Gamble house still stood,
And though the porch hung askew and the eaves all drooped,
I thought whoever lived there to be the luckiest in town.
I often imagined how I'd spend a crisp autumn morning
With a book under an elm tree, out of sight of the road
Where I sometimes saw the fog glow at sunrise.
It would likely be impossible to read there –
I'd probably lie back to study the tangled amber limbs above or
Jump up to run into the woods.
Who would ever need to escape on a page if they
Owned that storybook expanse?

It wasn't until my teen years that I learned why
Heaven's executors could justify letting the walls rot,
Why neighbors' signs begged someone to
Save it when the wrecking crews were called.
My dad and I ventured up the driveway the
Weekend before they came.
Camera in hand, I archived the details while the
Rolling hills' old enchantment faded like the paint.
I was in class two blocks away when it was razed.

It was always eerie to see the sidewalk leading nowhere, the
Roof of the barn and caretaker's house through the trees.
There were other ways we could drive.
After all the fantasized magic, it sounds wrong to say I
Forgot it, but eventually, I didn't think to walk there,
Didn't register whose woods those were behind
Lischer and that deer on the knoll.
It was chance when traffic detoured us past it and I
Gasped at the new city park sign underneath nine years of growth.
Two weeks later when a wood chipper parked beside my drive to
Destroy the neighbor's tree and my off-day morning,
I shut down the laptop and put on my gym shoes.

There were years I used to say I

Lived in Cheviot instead of Westwood.

We were right on the border, so it didn't really matter,

And the blocks around my high school lost their last verdant

Figments when the Sisters sold the halls.

I assumed those Secret Gardens were confined to

Childhood memory – a perception of a purer mind.

But it was real that day I laid beneath the elm trees,

Topaz leaves landing where a porch once stood.

Cinnamon

You might think I just received a
Text from a crush, the way I'm
Clutching the phone with crinkled eyes,
But actually, I've only checked the weather.
Humming a folk song under my breath,
I unfold the burnt-orange cable-knit sweater
From the shelf where it's waited ten months,
And I sigh with delight at the cotton's embrace,
As blissful as the first time I shed sleeves in March.

A quick granola bar suffices most of the year, but I
Have to make breakfast in October.
I leave the side door open as I peel and cut the apples,
Stealing glances at the neighbor's red maple tree.
I melt the butter in the oldest pan, though it
Takes a bit longer to clean –
There are many unpractical rules like this in autumn that
Aren't upheld by those who care if they make sense.
Like the amount of cinnamon I'm stirring into the sugar
When I shook even more into my mug.
I do the same with lavender in April.

I flip a pancake on the second burner as the
Fruit caramelizes on the first,
And I throw some pecans on the final assemblage before
Taking the plate and half-sipped coffee to the porch.
The air fills my lungs in a way it can't in summer.
I sit for a moment with the dish on my lap,
Breathing with intention and inhaling the
Bittersweet scents as I wrap my fingers
Flush against the ceramic,
Not because they're particularly cold, but
Because it's such a comfort to be warmed.
As soothing as a glass of lemonade in May.

Sonder

There's a light on near the top of the
Phelps Hotel across the park,
Warm against the pale slate of a
Monday sky piercing the tissue so deep that
I can hardly hold my pen.

Who is this traveler shelling dimes out
In the Central Business District?
I know they're most likely an attorney whose
Assistant will bill the view to a client,
But that's a little too close to the reality I'll be
Returning to in fifteen minutes,
So I fill the space behind the drapes with a
Graying retired botanist
Pouring a fair trade brew into a chipped mug as she
Waits for a layer to dry on her easel.

The lingering scent of the morning's rain
Makes me imagine she's just been to Portland –
There's a buoy on her keychain and her
Notebooks are full of wharves.
She might be on her way to the Smokies

Or someplace warmer, like the Outer Banks,
But I'd prefer to think her calendar tiles are open,
With a single reminder two months ahead to
Visit her sister back home in Pennsylvania.

Or, if they're lucky, her sister will
Fly out to meet her somewhere near Route 66,
Ring the new year in by getting lost.
And they'll flip through the sketches together,
Making stories up for each vignette,
From the children playing tag along the beach
To the woman writing poems in the park.

Without Saying It

No one would notice if I kept these words to myself,
But this attempt at turning these
Last few years into art feels incomplete without
Acknowledging the fear that
Persistently slows my pen.
So I'll wince through a few more lines in the
Fading Sunday light and tell you what I've been
Trying to say without saying it –
I know that I waited too long.

The shift from prose to poetry was inevitable after
That morning I stumbled on Mary's "Wild Geese" and
Let twenty-five years run down my cheeks.
I've always hesitated to share my real life on paper.
I used to hide it in fiction,
Placing my own dreams in stronger women's hands.
Maybe they could get away with them.

I look back on some of these stories with a
Bright red pen aimed less at their syntax and
More at their audacity.
My experiences aren't all that significant.

I'm embarrassed by how long it's taken me to

Get places my peers have already passed.

And I'm still afraid, after ironing out my nerve,

That you'll pick up this book and laugh.

Because you know me.

And you knew the way things were.

There are photographs from concerts and road trips

Taped to the counter by my desk.

Sometimes, I catch a glimpse of my reflection in the

Windows of the skywalk and think, for just a second,

That there's a stranger walking beside me.

I'm finally starting to look my age.

I take Mary's *Devotions* to the park when the wisteria blooms.

She asks what I plan to do.

Time to Turn the Page

Back in those days I've told you about
Between graduation tassels and chocolate boxes when I
Found some crucial pages in the stark and infinite unknown,
My long August walks bled into September
And I listened, for the first time in eighteen years, as the
School bells rang without me.

I told my dad it was nice to be done with homework,
To throw away the flyers of notebook deals,
But I wore through my socks seeking respite on the pavement.
Out past Daytona to avoid the elementary traffic,
Down the hill by the drugstore and up to the fieldhouse on Robb.
I added more blocks; the mile stretched to four –
Life's a flat-line fever pitch when you have nowhere to go.

Two more interviews and two more slow rejections.
May's bright hopes dissolved with the list of prospects,
And my feet slowed on Applegate as I imagined my
Reflection in the eyes of a passing jogger and saw a
Sweat-sheened baby face in old tennis shoes –

Not a single clue I'd received a degree with honors
Or any of the other goals I'd built my sense of worth around.
To the passersby, I was just a nameless neighbor,

And the longer I sat with that image, the less its simplicity stung.
I stepped into the library with a grounded, sober clarity,
Checked out a memoir as a reader, not a student.
The yards on Manning stood out in sharper detail with
Yesterday's expectations set aside,
With everything but the present called into place,
With only one second to command.

So as I wiped my eyes that night, staring up into the dark,
I made a promise to dress at the crack of dawn,
To make a cup of tea and take the laptop outside,
Open Chapter Twelve where I'd left off back in June.
The future was uncertain and my confidence was low,
But I'd finish the book for myself, to know I could.

Deer in the Snow

There's a memory that wraps me in earth tones
Every time I hear late October's parting geese:
Wood grain basement walls cast gold by an amber lamp
Beside the rocker where my grandma hummed along to a
Score I'd heard a dozen times before,
Details a nine-year-old somehow knew to romanticize
That time she stayed the night and really focused on the
Lyrics in that penultimate scene whose
Thick cello chords would prevail
Across the years and miles and measures –

Taking me back to the hill at Harbin Park,
The bench where Grandma took a
Sketchbook one whole summer,
Promises to paint the vista that I already
Knew she couldn't keep,
Understanding, somehow, that it was okay to
Validate dreams she wouldn't reach,
To lean into the process with no end secured.

I cried when they painted over the
Flowers on the staircase,

The last art project ever finished.
They would never have sold the townhouse if they didn't,
But I couldn't stop thinking of how she'd
Climbed the ladder for weeks
To wind vines and petals through the
Portrait museum of her legacy.
How she'd take each guest
To the landing and
Identify each framed face
Years after the rest began to fade.

It was only after the stroke took her stories
That the nurses stopped hearing those seven names
And the grandchild and great grandchild count that stayed
Frozen for the final decade,
Yet she still smiled at any kids the nurses brought by.
I wonder if she ever mistook a
Neighbor's granddaughter as me.
I hope they replied that they missed her, too.

That November night was as slow and silent
As those last two and a half years.
I had to rummage through cupboards of photographs
To replace that waning image

With waterfalls and tandem bikes,
Banjos, picnics, and palms,
The only daughter given permission to
Walk past the gate.
Intrepid hazel tomboy
Who showed a four-year-old the
Patience she'd given twenty-two before
As they turned the sun into faces with crayons
Down I-75 and back.

I wear one of her old turquoise rings
To remember that rambling painter
And promise the same joie de vivre.
It's one of many things that came my way
While they pried up the tiles and boxed up the halls.
There's a seashell lamp on my dresser,
Glass floats in the attic,
But when they asked me what I wanted,
The only thing I said was the
Painting in the upstairs guest room,
There since I was five:
Three deer grazing in the snow,
Heads and antlers only pencil,
Waiting for their artist to remember.

I've considered taking the time
To match the paint of their bodies
And carefully follow her guide,
But they remain unfinished,
Free to roam inside the
Inspirations of another year.
Dreams begun for the sake of dreaming.
A song you can't recall the end to,
That wanders everywhere
But its final note.

These Nights

Late revelations wander in to catch me on the
Edge of sleep and whisper eleven words
I know I'll lose before morning.
My sigh is gentle,
Hand unwinding from the blankets to
Stroke the shelf beside me in the dark
Until I feel the leathery cover of my book and
Cool, slick clip of my pen.
I pull aside the drape above my head for light, but the
Moon's just a sliver tonight,
So I crack open the cover and glide my fingers
Over the indentations of Aunt Kathy's inscription:
Write something beautiful today.
The pages fall with ease past several months of riffs.
I stop when they cease to bend and search their
Surfaces for valleys, only to
Flip a few more out of caution,
Clicking the cartridge into place to
Scrawl the evening's peace across the page with
All the grace and precision of a
Kindergartner learning with crayon.

Whether I can decipher them in the morning is moot;

The words are out,

Captured in ink instead of my brain.

And in returning my book to its place,

The mattress dissipates to consume me like a cloud,

One final revelation kissing me goodnight:

That these nights are, perhaps,

My favorite poems of all.

Surrender

A brief amber flash shines in Sammie's eyes as a
Log shifts in the fire, sending a quick
Spray of sparks into the cold October sky.
Our laughter quiets for a second into twin contented sighs,
And I marvel aloud, for the hundredth time,
At the endless sea of stars.
It's a scene I've written since I was a child,
Since about the time that eight-year-old asked
If I wanted to join her club at ballet.

It was easy to find her in the woman who
Stepped away from the stove this evening to
Dance around the cabin's tiny kitchen.
Yesterday, we took pictures on a red covered bridge
Like we used to capture moments in her backyard as teens.
She's the same girl I've walked around countless stores with,
Who cried with me in a stadium, dressed in pink.
But she's also someone new, someone growing,
A person every chapter designed her to be.

Our stories pause as she picks up the braided sweetgrass she
Bought at an incense shop in town.

Her hand rests, for a moment, on her stomach as she
Murmurs intentions for her daughter.
As she throws the braid in the fire, I think of the
Months she'd longed for that news.
This trip was supposed to be, in part, a
Recovery from summer's disappointments;
I was grateful it became a celebration.

Still, the remnant of a soft ache returns when she takes a
Handful of herbs and, after prayers for her family,
Asks that I receive all I want this next year.
A loon calls from across the lake as her
Hand releases the leaves,
The low notes blending with John Denver's voice floating
Gently from the speaker in the grass.

It's a song I played this afternoon as I watched the
Sun turn the golden trees a deeper shade of auburn.
I looked down at the metal mug of coffee in my hands,
The lawn chair and orange flannel shirt,
And I sat back to watch as six years of daydreams
Settled into one perfect image before me,
My paper world brought to life.

The lavender and rosemary crack and spark in the flames,
And as I take the bag from Sammie, she
Asks what it is I want from the coming year.
Two nights ago, I might have stumbled over
Stale romantic visions and pursuits I've lost faith in,
The doubtful somedays in my savings account.
I hear the wind touch the boughs above the water as I
Shake the dried leaves into my hand and
Inhale their sharp, sweet scent.

The strings fade in the speaker as I toss the
Herbs into the embers with a smile.

From the Space Between Songs

November's dawn sets the clouds above my tea ablaze
And highlights the copper buried in my hair.
There's a soft flavor to these mornings,
A soundless settling into the season as the
Sun peeks through fresh-bared branches to
Lend gentle warmth to a crisp, pale scene.
The roads nearby rush headlong from
Brilliant oranges and rich harvests to
Bold reds and taffeta bows,
But I want to linger here a little longer
In the quiet brown.

Across the street, a Cooper's hawk perches on a
Bough obscured a week ago.
Her catch is parting southward or burrowing in;
She doesn't seem to mind.
Her eyes point eastward,
Savoring the golden silence with me.
Maybe she's just resigned herself to the
Approaching dead of winter,
Or maybe she feels the reverberations of

Something low and steady
Rising from the shorn earth,
Sinking into the space between songs –
The deep inhalation before a new phrase begins,
The moment you pause and remember
What you're meant to say.

Acknowledgements

These acknowledgements could easily stretch into ten pages if I don't rein myself in – each time I start to draft them, I'm reminded of more wonderful folks who have mentored and encouraged me through the years. Many of them inspired these poems.

Thank you first to my parents, Rick and M'Lissa. I'm immensely grateful for your support of all my pursuits, and for instilling in me the value of curiosity. Thank you also to my grandparents, whose legacies continue to guide me – Richard, Garlan, Wilfred, Viola, and Bill.

Thank you to the teachers and professors who helped me turn writing from a pastime into a passion, including Mrs. Nan Wells, Dr. Elizabeth Mason, Prof. Jeffrey Hillard, Mr. Scott Kramer, Dr. Elizabeth Bookser Barkley, and Dr. Peter Robinson. Thank you to my many mentors beyond the classroom, particularly Tim and Julie.

Thank you to my friends who turn each day into poetry, especially Sammie, Morgan, Cat, and Jessica. I can't imagine these past "in-between" years without your love.

A special thank you to my friend Cat Rider, who asked if she could take my author headshot someday when this was just a distant dream. I'm incredibly honored to have your beautiful artwork on this cover, and to have your presence in my life.

My grateful acknowledgement to my favorite poet, Mary Oliver, whose poems "Wild Geese" (1986) and "The Summer Day" (1990) I reference in "Without Saying It," as well as her 2017 anthology *Devotions: The Selected Poems of Mary Oliver*, published by Penguin Press. My gratitude also to Paul McCartney, John Lennon, and the Beatles, whose 1970 song "The Long and Winding Road" I reference in "Bittersweet," and to Frances Hodgson Burnett, whose 1911 book *The Secret Garden* I reference in "Westwood."

Finally, my deep appreciation to the journals that first published the following poems:

"Choir of Bones" – *Plumwood Mountain Journal*

"Downy" – *300 Days of Sun*

"Electric Ghosts" – *The Poet's Touchstone*

"From the Space Between Songs" – *Mantis*

"Margins" – *Mantis*

"Overgrown" – *300 Days of Sun*

"Reckless Hymn" – *Common Threads*

"The Way It Was Supposed to Be" – *300 Days of Sun*

Photo by Cat Rider

Carolyn Kesterman is a proud Westsider of Cincinnati, Ohio who has been filling notebooks with prose and poetry ever since her fourth grade teacher encouraged her to write stories with her weekly spelling words. She obtained her Bachelor of Arts degree in English with a concentration in creative writing from Mount St. Joseph University in 2018, and wrote feature articles for the Sisters of Charity of Cincinnati during two internships in their Communications Office. Her short fiction has been published in several journals, including the *Notre Dame Review*.

After spending three years drafting a novel that she still plans to publish someday, her writing pursuits changed direction when she added line breaks to the notes in her phone and fell in love with poetry. Ten of her poems have been published in journals, including *Mantis*, *The Poet's Touchstone*, and *Open Minds Quarterly*. She is a member of the Ohio Poetry Association.

For six years, she has worked as a legal administrative assistant at a law firm in downtown Cincinnati. Many of her favorite pastimes can be found on these pages, such as hiking, gardening, and of course, listening to music.

www.ingramcontent.com/pod-product-compliance
Lightning Source LLC
Chambersburg PA
CBHW020548030426
42337CB00013B/1011